Narrative Theology As A Hermeneutic Approach

Narrative Theology As A Hermeneutic Approach

David Hampton

ISBN 978-0-557-09996-2

Lulu Publishers

www.lulu.com

To
Taylor and Gabriel

Contents

Preface

This work was hewn out of love and as a student of preaching and theology. The more I learn, the more I realize how much I do not know! While a seminary student at Christian Theological Seminary in 1996, I developed an affinity for the Narrative aspect of biblical hermeneutics because of its attention to the language of the text and its treatment of the Bible as one continuous story about God. Thus, the context and nexus of all scripture is centered upon Jesus Christ. I did not write with the intent to reach a particular audience, however, I hope that anyone who reads this book will be inspired to think critically, and might appreciate the detail that narrative theology lends to biblical scholarship. I am ever grateful to my wife and children, my family, my seminary professors, my parishioners – past and present, my colleagues in ministry, the City of Indianapolis, and the Borough of Brooklyn.

Introduction:

The Use of Narrative Hermeneutics in Theology

The Importance of Intratextualism

Narrative theology is a fairly new development and has had a major impact on much English-language theology since the early 1970s. The basic feature of narrative theology is the particular attention it pays to narratives, or stories, in relation to Christian theology. Narrative theology is based on the observation that the Bible tells stories about God as well as making doctrinal and theological statements.

Hans Frei has pointed out that the Enlightenment of the eighteenth century reduced theology to general rational concepts that led to a disregard for the narrative quality of the biblical text. Another proponent of narrative theology is Paul Ricoeur, who maintains that there is something of crucial importance to be interpreted in the fullness of biblical language. He begins with the "assumption that this kind if discourse is not senseless, that it is worthwhile to analyze it, because something is said that is not said by other kinds of discourse."[1] I will discuss Frei and Ricoeur, their hermeneutics, and their points of convergence and divergence concerning narrative theology.

The appeal of narrative theology is such that it will be attractive to those concerned with reclaiming the centrality of scripture in modern theology. It is my contention that when scripture becomes the focal point of one's theological reflection, barriers of all kinds can be expunged and eliminated, such as denominational, spiritual, and cultural barriers that create division among Christians.

---

[1] Paul Ricoeur, "Philosophy of Religious Language," *Journal of Religion* 54 (1974): 71.

Allister McGrath offers a very helpful list of advantages to narrative theology which provides five points:

1. Narrative is the main literary type or genre found in scripture.

2. The approach avoids the dulling sense of abstraction found in much academic theological writing.

3. Narrative theology affirms that God meets us in history and speaks to us as one who has been involved in history.

4. Recognition of the narrative character of scripture allows us to appreciate how scripture effectively articulates the tension between the limited knowledge of the human characters in the story and the omniscience of God.

5. Narrative theology focuses its attention upon the literary structure of scripture rather than the subjective historical factors, thus alleviating needless argument over whether an event actually occurred or is true. It focuses on the meaning behind the text and the importance it has in regard to our Christian identity.

Mark Wallace proposes that the task of theology is to "uncover the grammar that has always guided the church's experience and specify its applicability to particular theological problems and concerns."[2] Wallace also states that intratextual theology describes reality "within the scriptural framework rather than translating scripture into extra-scriptural categories."[3] Hans Frei argues that liberal interpretations of scripture tend to conform a biblical text around another world and another story, while the task of narrative theology is to incorporate a world or story into the biblical story, thus focusing on the authority and purpose of the scripture.

---

[2] Mark Wallace, *The Second Naiveté* (Macon, GA: Mercer University Press, 1990) 90.
[3] Ibid., 90.

The basis of this book (and the major argument that I have in favor of narrative theology) is that much of modern theology has neglected its fidelity to the biblical world in favor of articulating the relevant meanings of the Christian witness to contemporary culture. By engaging in intratextual theology (strict adherence to the text) and properly using the grammar of the text (correctly speaking about God), one can eliminate erroneous assertions made about the Word of God and the use of noncontextual foundations for faith that cause confusion.

Story and Systematic Theology

In the book *Why Narrative*, Stanley Hauerwas and David Burrell offer discourse on the systematic nature of story along with David Ford. This section will explain some of the dynamics of narrative theology as it relates to rationality in ethics and systematic theology.

I begin with the perspectives of Stanley Hauerwas and David Burrell in which they discuss the ethical aspects of narrative theology in the essay *From System to Story: An Alternative Pattern for Rationality in Ethics*. Their beginning argument states that "in the interest of securing a rational foundation for morality, contemporary ethical theory has ignored or rejected the significance of narrative for ethical reflection."[4] Their contention is that there has been a mistake on the part of contemporary ethical theory, which results in a distorted account of moral experience.

The question arises as to whether or not narrative is sufficient to take on all the issues that contemporary ethical theory cannot. Could it be that narrative simply offers another perspective due to its fresh and illuminating method of utilizing story for critical reflection? I cannot provide a single answer that will satisfy such an inquiry. However, I feel that story offers one of the most concise methods for critical reflection—especially theological reflection.

---

[4] Stanley Hauerwas and David Burrell, *Why Narrative*, (Eugene, OR: Wipf and Stock Publishers, 1997) 179.

Hauerwas and Burrell share a similar view with David Ford regarding the effectiveness of the systematic nature of narrative theology. Hauerwas and Burrell note the importance of language as a systematic set of connections between actions and characters, which offers a setting or syntax for subsequent responses. "Since character cannot be presented independently of the story or stories that develop it, the connection between the syntactical system and the way in which the language embodies a form of life, becomes crystal clear."[5]

By attending to character and a linguistic approach, stories will reveal themselves to us without any need for philosophical reminders or elaborate "eisegetical fabrications" (imposing a meaning into a text). The effectiveness of this approach is similar to that of an expository interpretation, but with an "epexegesis" or a more in-depth analysis of a biblical text. David Ford elaborately states that the "cultural-linguistic approach to Christian theology involves the *coinherence or perichoresis* of system, story, and performance, together with an accompanying ad hoc apologetics."[6] This approach adheres strictly to the context of the biblical narrative. Ford further states that, "both system and performance must be in continual, critical interaction with the story if it is to maintain its rational, moral, and spiritual integrity, and in this exchange apologetics takes place."[7] The mode of rationality must be appropriate to the content. Ford has sided with George Lindbeck as he too suggests that doctrines are not primarily truth claims or expressive symbols but are communally authoritative rules of discourse, attitude, and action.

Narrative and Christian Identity

In this section, I will offer a brief discussion on narrative theology as it relates to Christian identity. One of the more compelling discussions on narrative and identity that I have

---

[5] Ibid., 179.

[6] Ibid., 214–215.

[7] Ibid., 191.

read is by Alasdair MacIntyre in *Why Narrative* by Hauerwas. MacIntyre maintains that one cannot characterize behavior independently of intentions, nor can intentions be characterized independently of intelligible settings. MacIntyre refers to Aristotelian thought on the agent as both an actor and an author in a life narrative. This philosophical idea holds that humans enter upon a stage, which they did not design. Each person is his or her own main character but plays subordinate roles in the dramatic narratives of others, while each drama constrains the others. Thus, there is no present without some image of the future presenting itself in the form of a telos or a variety of ends or goals. It is out of this praxeology that MacIntyre develops the concept of personal identity.

Narrative can be effective in adequately articulating personal identity. Narrative would explain that such behavior as depression, suicide, or low self-image is characteristic of life becoming unintelligible and lacking a positive telos or any hope toward a positive future or end. From this perspective, our very being or ontological essence becomes a narrative based upon certain perceptions that can be changed either positively or negatively.

I contend that regardless of a person's or community's historical identity, Christian narrative can provide a new identity that is centered on the Word of God and the *logos* or personal manifestation of God in Jesus Christ. Such a hermeneutic eliminates the guilt of the past or differences that exist in this new identity.

The Narrative Hermeneutics of Hans Frei

The fundamental basis from which to begin to characterize the hermeneutic approach of Hans Frei can be found within his early dissertation on Karl Barth.[8] Though he developed this discussion early in his career, Frei's premise has remained the

---

[8] Hans Frei, *The Doctrine of Revelation in the Thought of Karl Barth,* (dissertation, New Haven: Yale University, 1956) 439.

same—the "absolute priority, independence, and sovereignty of the grace of God in regard to our knowledge of God."[9]

Hans Frei holds to similar convictions as Karl Barth, especially in the area of the authority of scripture. It would be safe to say that the fundamental characteristic of Barth's theology is that scriptural authority is centrally based and founded upon the Word of God. "Barth's theology seeks to be theonomously governed by its free submission to the Word of God—the center of Christian theology that is not something under our control, but something which exercises control over us."[10] Barth himself states, "We will not ask: why the Bible? and look for external grounds and reasons. We will leave it to the Bible itself ... to vindicate itself by what takes place [in it]."[11] Thus, the major axiom around which Frei bases his theology is that scripture need not be aligned with secular or extra-biblical sources of information to be substantiated, legitimated, or even interpreted.

William Placher points out that Frei's narrative hermeneutic approach is such that in "Christian theology, the story is the meaning of the doctrine, not the other way around. Christians do not figure out the real meaning of the biblical narratives in some doctrinal formulation and then discard the stories, but doctrines serve as aids for reflection on the biblical narratives."[12] Thus, it is the story that remains the central focus of understanding and meaning in a text, while the doctrinal (communally adopted teaching of the text) serves merely to illuminate the story for further practical application or theological reflection.

Another defining characteristic of Frei's theology is his position on historicity or the historical-critical method of biblical

---

[9] James Fodor, *Christian Hermeneutics,* (New York: Clarendon Press Oxford, 1995) 261.

[10] Mark Wallace, *Second Naiveté,* (Macon, GA: Mercer University Press, 1990) 4.

[11] Karl Barth, *Church Dogmatics,* (13 volumes Edinburgh: T. & T. Clark, 1936–1969).

[12] William Placher, *Narratives of a Vulnerable God,* (Westminster John Knox Press, 1994) 40.

interpretation. The theological framework for the authority of scripture is such that scripture is *history-like* rather than *like history*. Frei argues this point in his book *Eclipse of Biblical Narrative*. Frei's fundamental argument is that the "subtle transformation of historical consciousness which began in the eighteenth and nineteenth centuries and persists to the present mistakenly succeeded in identifying or equating the meaning of a narrative with its ostensive reference."[13] Frei contends that a problem exists concerning the rise in interests in areas of historicity, truth, and reference regarding scripture. In other words, the interpretive problem occurs when there is a presumption or question of historical accuracy of a story, thus relegating the meaningfulness of scripture to the accuracy of its historical reference. However, the meaning and reference of a history-like narrative primarily involves the way it renders a character's identity.

The Narrative Hermeneutics of Paul Ricoeur

Paul Ricoeur's hermeneutic approach has been shaped largely by his orientation and experience in philosophy. Ricoeur was born in Valence, France, on February 27, 1913, and graduated with a degree in philosophy from the Sorbonne in 1935. He studied German philosophy and theology in a German POW camp during World War II. It was there that he was influenced and able to study he works of Immanuel Kant, G. W. F. Hegel, Edmund Husserl, Rudolph Bultmann, and Karl Barth. Some of Ricoeur's earlier interests include his works and writings in existential philosophy as he provides an analysis of Husserl's phenomenology. Ricoeur aligns himself with Husserl in that "the value of phenomenological method lies in its description of consciousness to be a consciousness of something, a moving outside of oneself to the object or phenomenon intended."[14]

Ricoeur is a proponent of literary theory; thus he has formulated a narrative hermeneutic that is reflective of such. In

---

[13] James Fodor, *Christian Hermeneutics,* (New York: Clarendon Oxford Press, 1995) 262.
[14] Paul Ricoeur, *Figuring the Sacred,* (Minneapolis: Fortress Press, 1995) 3.

his own words, Ricoeur states, "Whatever ultimately may be the nature of religious experience—it comes to language, it is articulated in a language, and the most appropriate place to interpret it on its own terms is to inquire into its linguistic expression."[15] Mark Wallace has pointed out that in his efforts to provide theological-literary interpretive methods, Ricoeur seeks to make some sense of the different literary genres within the Bible. Ricoeur proposes that "scripture is a cross-fertilization between different literary genres and their corresponding theological itineraries preserves the polyphony of biblical revelation, the phenomenon of intertextuality in which different aspects of the divine revealing are given full play."[16]

Another significant characteristic of Ricoeur's narrative hermeneutic is his relational understanding between general and specific hermeneutics. General hermeneutics refers to philosophy, while special hermeneutics refers to theology. The defining mark of Ricoeur's hermeneutic approach is his priority of the use of philosophy over theology.

Plan, Purpose, and Proposal

Up to this point, I have attempted to lay the groundwork or foundation of the two narrative hermeneutic approaches of Hans Frei and Paul Ricoeur. What I plan to propose is a comparison of their respective approaches on specific areas of interest. While I cannot provide an exhaustive analysis, the areas of focus will concern four uses of narrative based upon the methods of Frei and Ricoeur: theological, theoretical, philosophical, and practical uses. It will be most interesting to discover where the two converge and diverge on these various issues concerning biblical interpretation. Even to this point, there are some obvious differences in the narrative philosophies of Frei and Ricoeur. My intent is not to play one against the other or to attempt to find which approach is the most effective; however, I will assess their respective strengths and weaknesses. I will also provide a

---

[15] Ibid., 35.
[16] Mark Wallace, *Second Naiveté*, (Macon, GA: Mercer University Press, 1990) 40.

thoughtful analysis of the methodologies of Frei and Ricoeur, who have been viewed as having opposing ideologies. Their narrative styles will be evident throughout the discussions on the various issues and topics.

Part I

Theological Uses

Frei and Ricoeur:
Story and Systematic Theology

Aside from the critical analysis that will be discussed concerning story and system in this section, my intent is also to provide some enlightenment on the ways in which our Christian identity can best be illuminated. "It is suggested that in Christian systematic theology *story* has a key role, inseparable from the form and content of the Christian stories, especially the Gospels."[2] In other words, the story is the focal point of the theological system and is in continual interaction with each category of the system.

The story provides the spiritual integrity and basis for the system. Therefore, when engaging in a discussion of any category of systematic theology, there must be a common core within the framework of the discussion, an intertwining (perichoresis) of the story and the system. This section will use this perichoresis of system and story as the springboard from which to engage in discussion on interpretive narrative, revelation, and Christology. My intent is to show how Frei and Ricoeur, though different in approach, maintain the same level of integrity and focus concerning the story in these three areas of theology.

Interpretive Narrative

I begin the discussion with Ricoeur's definition of interpretive narrative. Ricoeur postulates that this type of narrative is one in

---

[2] Stanley Hauerwas and David Burrell, *Why Narrative,* (Eugene, OR: Wipf and Stock Publishers, 1997) 191.

which the interpretive ideal is not merely placed strategically by the narrator, but that it is inextricably bound and incorporated into the narrative itself. "These are narratives in which the ideological interpretation these narratives wish to convey is not superimposed on the narrative by the narrator but is, instead, incorporated into the very strategy of the narrative."[3] The focal point of Ricoeur's approach lies in the primary understanding that, if a text is one with an interpretive function (similar to a midrash), then the juncture between exegesis and theology already functions in the text. This interpretive function exists before the exegetical-theological work of interpretation is applied to the text. Ricoeur characterizes this type of ideological interpretation *kerygma*. The kerygma functions in close association with theology in terms of the message being conveyed and the understanding of that message.

Ricoeur uses the passion narratives to illustrate this interpretive ideology. He states, "My question is whether the passion narratives have a comparable function, as regards the close imbrication of theology within the narratives, and whether the problem is not to bring into relation the theological function and the narrative structure."[4] His proposal is that the most elaborate feature of the Gospel narratives lies in the union between the kerygmatic function and the narrative aspects.

He further asserts that what he is attempting to reconstruct between a "narrativized kerygma" and a "kerygmatized narrative" seems to have its rationale in the identity proclaimed between the Christ of faith and the Jesus of history. Ricoeur mentions Hans Frei's book, *The Identity of Christ*, as he makes reference to the question, "Who do you say that I am?"[5] Ricoeur maintains that the function of interpretive narrative is to answer this Messianic question "through the combined interplay of plot and character development (as has been well known since

---

3 Paul Ricoeur, *Figuring the Sacred*, (Minneapolis: Fortress Press ,1995) 181.
4 Ibid., 183.
5 Hans Frei, *The Identity of Jesus Christ*, (Philadelphia: Fortress Press, 1974).

Henry James' reflections on *The Art of Fiction*)."[6] Clearly, this approach maintains Ricoeur's premise and use of literary theory along with maintaining the integrity of the story, which is the very basis of what is to be interpreted.

In 1982, Hans Frei and Paul Ricoeur lectured at Haverford College on theology interpretation of narrative hermeneutics. The nature of the lecture was such that each presented a response to the other's theological perspectives. In the book *Theology and Narrative*, William Placher and George Hunsinger have provided an edited version of Frei's lecture. Their argument in this book is such that they propose a methodological independence for theology as Hans Frei's ideas resonate with the idea of this methodology in his discussions.

Frei presents his discussion with two fundamental bases of thought concerning his narrative approach: (1) a philosophically based German approach called *Wissenschaft*, and (2) interpretation as being a particular activity within the Christian community. Placher and Hunsinger both support the latter as having greater significance. In the debate, Frei contends with Paul Ricoeur and David Tracy concerning the narrative character of biblical texts. Frei felt that Ricoeur, though a proponent of narrative interpretation, maintained a hermeneutic that possessed flaws. The major criticism of Ricoeur's methodology was his adherence and loyalty to philosophical interpretive functions vis-à-vis thoroughgoing theological interpretation. In other words, Frei's point of departure from the ideas of Ricoeur's concerns Ricoeur's adherence to *intertextuality* versus *intratextuality* (strict adherence to the text).

> Ricoeur and Tracy, Frei maintained, were still finally treating the Gospel stories about Jesus as presentations of a certain mode-of-being-in-the-world rather than, first of all, as narratives about the singular person of Jesus. They understood Jesus' selfhood primarily as an internal consciousness

---

[6] Paul Ricoeur, *Figuring the Sacred,* (Minneapolis: Fortress Press, 1995) 185.

expressed in words and deeds rather than as constituted by his enacted intentions.[7]

The major point of divergence between Hans Frei and Paul Ricoeur is that Frei finds it troublesome that Ricoeur's hermeneutic approach gives more priority to philosophy than to theology (more attention to general than to special hermeneutics). "Frei espouses a far more radically intratextual hermeneutic than Ricoeur. Whereas Ricoeur still wishes to retain some referential notion to account for text-world relations, Frei argues that since everything is text and textuality is everything, no recourse to reference is necessary."[8] I will return to the above point later in Part Two of the thesis.

Revelation

"In Christian faith revelation is always the revelation of God's Word. But what do Christians mean by God's Word and how does this word become a reality in contemporary experience?"[9] George Stroup maintains that the answer to these questions would require further explanation from Christology and pneumatology. The issue is that questions about the relation between the nature of God's Word and human words are actually obscured inquiries of Christians concerning the incarnation. Questions concerning how God's Word becomes reality in contemporary experience inevitably lead to Christian discussions on the Spirit and how Christ is made present in the world.

"The relation between God's Word and human words, therefore, is closely related to traditional christological issues that surround the doctrine of the incarnation."[10] So then, what role does Christian narrative play in light of revelation? It is the

---

[7] Hans Frei, *Theology and Narrative,* (New York: Oxford University Press, 1995) 117.

[8] James Fodor, *Christian Hermeneutics,* (New York: Oxford Press, 1995) 296.

[9] George Stroup, *The Promise of Narrative Theology,* (Eugene, OR: Wipf and Stock, 1997) 240.

[10] Ibid., 240.

center, or context, in which God's Word is heard in the midst of human words.

In *Essays on Biblical Interpretation,* Paul Ricoeur discusses revelation in such a way that he seeks to present the concept of revelation as well as the concept of reason. Ricoeur proposes that though revelation and reason do not necessarily concur or maintain the same exact function or position, both can enter into a dialogue as they, together, generate an understanding of faith. He structures his argument in such a way that revelation is expressed in many different ways and categories. There are five modes of discourse concerning revelation introduced by Ricoeur: Prophetic, Narrative, Prescriptive, Wisdom, and Hymnic. A brief description of each is in order; however, my point of emphasis will be a discussion on narrative discourse.

Ricoeur maintains that prophetic discourse should serve as the primary basis of reference concerning revelation. The nature of prophecy is such that the prophet speaks not in his own name but in the name of another. "So here the idea of revelation appears as identified with the idea of a double author of speech and writing. Revelation is the speech of another behind the speech of the prophet."[11]

I will provide a more in-depth example of the approach that Ricoeur uses regarding narrative discourse. Ricoeur demonstrates a literary-critical approach as he provides an exegetical work by Gerhard von Rad in which he uncovers the language of Deuteronomy 26:5-10.

> My Father was a wandering Aramaean. He went down to Egypt to find refuge there, few in numbers; but there he became a nation, great, mighty, and strong. The Egyptians ill-treated us, they gave us no peace and inflicted harsh slavery on us. But we called on Yahweh the God of our fathers. Yahweh heard our voice and saw our misery, our toil and our oppression; and Yahweh

---

[11] Paul Ricoeur, *Essays on Biblical Interpretation,* (Philadelphia: Fortress Press, 1980) 75.

> brought us out of Egypt with a mighty hand and outstretched arm, with great terror, and with signs and wonders. He brought us here and gave us this land, a land where milk and honey flow. Here then I bring the firstfruits of the produce of the soil that you, Yahweh, have given me. (Jerusalem Bible)

Ricoeur first points out how the recitation "designates Yahweh in the third person, as the supreme actant, then raises to an invocation that addresses God in the second person. ('Here then I bring the firstfruits of the produce of the soil that you, Yahweh, have given me.')"[12] He then points out that the essential element concerning narrative discourse is the emphasis on the event(s) as the effect of God's act. Thus, the primary emphasis of the narrative is placed upon confession rather than inspiration. "God's mark is in history before being in speech. It is only secondarily in speech inasmuch as this history itself is brought to language in the speech-act of narration."[13]

Prescriptive discourse corresponds to the will of God. It encompasses a more practical dimension of revelation. Ricoeur contends that the prescriptive idea of revelation is problematic, especially in light of the traditional understanding of revelation.

> In this regard, the translation, beginning with the Septuagint, of the word *Torah* by *nomos* or law is completely misleading. It leads us, in effect, to enclose the idea of an imperative from above within the idea of a divine law...If we transcribe the idea of an imperative in terms of Kant's moral philosophy, we are more and more constrained to lean the idea of revelation on that of heteronomy; that is, to express it in terms of submission to a higher, external command. The

---

12 Ibid., 79.
13 Ibid., 79.

idea of dependence is essential to the idea of revelation, but really to understand this originary dependence within the orders of speaking, willing, and being, we must first criticize the ideas of heteronomy and autonomy both as taken together and as symmetrical to each other.[14]

Wisdom discourse is a literary expression found in wisdom literature (i.e., Proverbs); however, Ricoeur asserts that it surpasses every literary genre. Wisdom is the element of revelation that adds to a deeper understanding of the Law and the Word of God. It must be understood within the context and framework of prophetic, narrative, and prescriptive discourses. "Wisdom overflows the framework of the Covenant, which is also the framework of the election of Israel and the promise made to Israel...Wisdom does not teach us how to avoid suffering, or how to magically deny it...it teaches us how to endure, how to suffer suffering."[15]

Hymnic discourse is best exemplified by the Psalms. There are three major genres that constitute hymnic discourse: hymns of praise, supplication, and thanksgiving. Ricoeur further asserts that celebration or praise actually elevates the story and turns it into an invocation.

Christology and the Logic of Christ

As stated early on, my intent in this section on story and systematic theology is to provide some enlightenment on how our Christian identity can best be illuminated. Before engaging in a discussion of the methodologies of Frei and Ricoeur on christological issues, I will first provide some preliminary discourse on the person and work of Jesus Christ. Who, in fact, is Jesus Christ? The question has been asked for nearly two thousand years and has been expounded upon by many

---

[14] Ibid., 82.
[15] Ibid., 86

theologians and biblical scholars. As I have learned from the biblical text in Mark, Jesus is the Son of God. He is divinity with us now and was adopted for divine purpose. The very name of Christ means *anointed one*, placing Jesus in the category of one who is an agent of that divine purpose. He is characterized also as the Son of Man, meaning that he is the divine judge of man sent from God (actually the person of God). The name Jesus means *savior*, so Jesus is the Messiah and Savior of the world.

Some classical affirmations about Jesus Christ should be noted, as they have been adopted by the church to facilitate our human understanding of Jesus Christ. In this analysis of classical Christology, it should be noted that these views are not without problems. What does Classical Christology seek to affirm? It sought to provide a working definition of Christ in relation to death, idolatry, and sin. The conclusions were that Jesus is the "life of the world (who delivers us from death, the light of the world (who delivers us from ignorance), and the savior of the world (who redeems us from sin)"[16]

Some of the heresies that existed understood Jesus as only having the appearance of being human or that Jesus was not the incarnate God but a created image of God. Plato and Arius were two instrumental figures who provided these thoughts; the Gnostics and Docetists denied the full humanity of Jesus Christ and are arguably the oldest and most persistent christological heresies in the church.

Classical Christology was an attempt to respond with some intelligible solutions and explanations of the nature of Jesus Christ. The affirmation of the classical school of thought occurred at the councils of Nicea (325), Constantinople (381) regarding the Trinity, Ephesus (431), and Chalcedon (451) regarding the two natures of Jesus Christ. Critics of classical thought maintain that these affirmations are obscure, abstract, and far removed from the experience of faith. It also loses sight of the historical reality of Jesus Christ and must be reinterpreted in order to encounter any ambiguity and speculative jargon.

---

[16] Taken from lecture notes in Systematic Theology, Clark Williamson, p.178.

Clark Williamson has developed a set of problems regarding classical Christology that I will summarize:

(a)   was expressed in terms that undercut the very symbol it sought to articulate

(b)   never overcame the problem of subordinationism

(c)   never gave a coherent account of how Jesus was fully human

(d)   was unable to articulate its faith without being anti-Judaic

(e)   was developed under a system of sacramental salvation and under the terms of the church.[17]

Despite the problems of classical Christology, the intent remains an essential part of any adequate Christology. This intent was to express the salvific presence of God in and through Jesus Christ.

Now that we have a definition of Christology provided within the context and framework of systematic theology, I will offer discourse from the basis of story. I will provide an analysis of the approaches of Frei and Ricoeur relating to the identity of Christ based upon their respective books: *The Identity of Jesus Christ* (Frei) and *Figuring the Sacred* (Ricoeur). In chapter 10 of *The Identity of Jesus Christ* Hans Frei discusses "The Enacted Intention of Jesus." Frei begins his discussion with the premise that the story of salvation is the story that is enacted by Jesus through obedience. "What we must now try to show is that the story, (not necessarily as history), should be taken in its own right and not symbolically and that, if it is read for its own sake, it suggests that Jesus' identity is self-focused and unsubstitutably his own."[18] Frei maintains that apart from the story of Jesus, we do not actually know much about Jesus. It is

---

17 Ibid., 180.
18 Hans Frei, *The Identity of Jesus Christ,* (Eugene, OR: Wipf and Stock Publishers, 1998) 145.

the story that we must rely heavily – if not totally – upon in order to know the intentions and identity of Jesus.

The primary intention of Jesus was to be perfectly obedient to God unto the point of death. "He was perfectly obedient, and his obedience to God was one with his intention to do what had to be done on men's behalf."[19] Up to this point, Frei maintains the hermeneutic approach consistent with the premise that the story provides the meaning of a specific doctrine rather than the doctrine giving meaning to the story. Frei is not so much concerned with proving the intentions of the historical Jesus. The focal point here is to provide information about the Jesus depicted in the story (narrative) and to use critical judgment based on the available evidence (if one so chooses to judge).

> Whether indeed the "historical" Jesus *intended* the crucifixion and in what sense whether he went freely to his death and with what motives, we cannot infer directly from the available evidence. The believer will, of course, find confirmation of the coming together of Jesus' intention and acts with those of God in God's raising him from the dead. He will claim that whatever Jesus' motives, the resurrection is the seal of God's confirmation upon them…The resurrection demonstrates Jesus' acceptability to God as being obedient to God's will. But the resurrection is not, of course, an event subject to critical historical judgment; and even if taken at face value, it, by itself, tells us little about the internal history of Jesus.[20]

Frei's point is that Jesus' intentions were confirmed by God based upon Jesus' obedience through the crucifixion. This confirmation was made manifest in the resurrection. "When we seek to determine what Jesus was like by identifying the enactment of his central intention, we note that who told the

---

[19] Ibid., 145.
[20] Ibid., 146.

story about him or commented on it speak of his obedience to God's *will* (*Rom. 5:19; Phil.2:8; Heb. 5:8*)."[21]

I have stressed some specific points in order to provide insight into Frei's hermeneutic approach regarding the identity of Jesus. There are three characteristics consistently present throughout Frei's discussion giving insight into his methodology. First, Frei maintains a biblical approach by which he yields to the authority of the biblical story. Second, Frei holds to a hermeneutic in which the story is the meaning of the doctrine, not the doctrine being the meaning of the story (see footnote 18). Third, Frei maintains an intratextual pattern of identification, finding all bases of inquiry about Jesus within the biblical texts or stories about Jesus (see footnote 21).

As Frei possesses a consistent pattern or hermeneutic approach in his discussion on the identity of Jesus Christ, Paul Ricoeur also maintains a set of methodological characteristics as he discusses the logic of Jesus. Somewhat similar to the subject matter of Frei in his discussion on the intention of Jesus Christ, Ricoeur offers discourse on the logical reasoning behind Jesus' actions in his book *Figuring the Sacred*.[22] Of course, Ricoeur makes use of a different set of methodological characteristics that are reflective of his hermeneutic approach. We will see those characteristics in the following discussion.

The primary argument that Ricoeur upholds in chapter sixteen of his book is that human logic is inherently different than the logic of Jesus (God) and even Paul (based upon biblical narrative). Ricoeur holds that human logic is a logic of equality, while the logic of Jesus, God, and Paul is a logic of excess or "superabundance."

> First, let us speak of human logic, of our logic. We can do this on the same ground, that of penal law and punishment, to which Paul introduces another logic. It is the virtue of penal law to fit, by always very exact proportions, the punishment to the

---

[21] Ibid., 146.

[22] Paul Ricoeur, *Figuring the Sacred,* (Minneapolis: Fortress Press, 1995).

crime. The ideal, according to the spirit of the law, would be that the penalty equals the mistake. In this admirable effort is summarized human logic; human logic is a logic of equality, of equivalence. But the logic of God, the logic of Jesus, the logic of Paul is quite another matter. This other logic is one of excess, of superabundance.[23]

Ricoeur explains the logic of superabundance, first within the context of Old Testament theology. Beginning with the Genesis story, the logic of equivalence is introduced through the flood. "The story begins as a myth of punishment (Gen. 6:5-7). The whole logic of punishment is contained here and in some way divinized."[24] Ricoeur maintains that out of the crime and punishment that occurred in Genesis, the logic of superabundance emerged in the manner of repentance to God. It is through the narratives of the New Testament that this logic is fully illuminated. Ricoeur refers to Matthew 5:39-42 with the statement, "You have heard it said." Through the use of literary analysis, Ricoeur points out that the rhetoric used within the text expresses this logic.

The ancient law says…"An eye for an eye and a tooth for a tooth." This famous law of the talion appears barbarous to us today. Ethnology teaches us, however, that it represents the first conquest over endless vengeance, the first measuring of the penalty to the size of the crime. But what impresses us is that this conquest of limited penalty is the imposition of the old logic of equivalence. And it is the logic that Jesus reverses. How? By giving, four times in a row, an extreme commandment that each time intrigues, perhaps revolts, and in any case distresses. Let us look closely at the rhetoric of the text. Jesus does

---

[23] Ibid., 279.
[24] Ibid., 279

> not proceed as moralists would do by giving a
> general rule. He begins each time with a limited
> situation, undoubtedly rare, surely improbable,
> and each time the act illuminates by what we
> would tend to call an overreaction.[25]

Ricoeur adheres to the statement that Jesus instructs or acts by means of the "exception" and not merely by means of the "rule." Herein lies the logic of superabundance. The question that arises now is whether or not this kind of logic leaves us with no sense of direction. "It seems to me that the situation here is the same as it is in other usages by Jesus of an extreme language, such as the extravagance of a parable or the hyperbole of a proverb: a log in the eye or a camel through the eye of a needle. Parables, paradoxes, hyperboles, and extreme commandments all *dis*orient only in order to *re*orient us.[26]

Ricoeur maintains that what is reoriented in us is our imaginations, which open us up to new and endless possibilities of seeing and discovering. Similar to the approach of Frei, Ricoeur uses an intratextual hermeneutic to illuminate and describe the logic of Jesus. Two points of divergence in their approaches are that Ricoeur makes use of literary critical analysis and also employs a much more philosophical approach to elaborate on the identity of Jesus through the idea of logic. Both possess strengths within their respective methods; however, the defining characteristics of both will only work within the context of their chosen topics. More specifically, Frei's use of strict biblical authority would not adequately express the logic of Jesus as Ricoeur discussed it using the method of literary analysis. At the same time, Ricoeur's philosophical approach would not be as effective if he were engaged in a narrative discussion of the identity of Jesus Christ as did Frei. It is important to note that Ricoeur proceeds in each discussion from a Christian base though he uses a philosophical method. Ricoeur seemingly yields to

---

[25] Ibid., 280.
[26] Ibid., 281.

biblical integrity and would say that where he cannot adequately argue from philosophy, the preacher can.

Through the categories of interpretive narrative, revelation, and the identity and logic of Jesus Christ, I have offered discourse on the methodological similarities and differences of Frei and Ricoeur. Both possess strengths in their hermeneutic approaches regarding story and systematic theological issues; however, I have concluded that weaknesses exist in this area only when one begins to engage in discussion from the perspective of the other, creating divergent ideologies. Naturally, there will be a different conclusion if one man takes a theological approach to a narrative and the other maintains a philosophical approach.

Part II

Theoretical Uses

Frei and Ricoeur:
Reference and Language Approaches to Hermeneutics

Literary Interpretation of Text

In this section, I will offer some insight into Ricoeur's use of literary-theological hermeneutics and the response to this approach by Hans Frei through a summary-analysis of Mark Wallace's book *Second Naiveté*. Wallace provides a discussion on Ricoeur's interest in maintaining some sense of balance between the varieties of biblical discourse and mixed genres that exist in modern day theology (narrative). "Ricoeur seeks a balance between the play of differences and the strategies of coherence within scripture. The Bible is a complicated intertext characterized by the interpretation of the competing genres and themes—not a stable book dominated by the Jesus story, as many narrative theologians maintain."[1]

The basis of Wallace's argument hinges upon the premise mentioned above. I will discuss Ricoeur's intertextual method of interpretation more in-depth, including a critique by Hans Frei, however, first the groundwork must be laid concerning Ricoeur's use of literary-theological interpretation. Wallace compares Ricoeur's approach with other types of narrative theology as he affirms that it is much different from many mainline narrative theologies. Karl Barth, as well as Hans Frei,

---

[1] Mark Wallace, *Second* Naiveté, (Macon, GA: Mercer University Press, 1990) 41.

holds to the assumption that all theology should be a retelling of the biblical stories.

> Ricoeur's biblical narratology is significantly different from current mainline narrative theologies. Unlike these approaches, Ricoeur's hermeneutic does not privilege (ironically) the genre of narrative as the principle medium through which the Bible communicated its message. Barth's argument that all theology *in nuce* should be a sustained retelling of the biblical sagas casts a long shadow over contemporary Christian theology and its concern with narrative. Ricoeur, however, wonders if this Barthian assumption does not have more to do with our fundamental love for coherent stories and dramas than it does with a balanced reading of the Bible in its conflicted play of multiple meanings and genres.[2]

Ricoeur employs a more *intertextual* hermeneutic approach to Scripture in which different means of revelation are given consideration. It is through the use of this method that Ricoeur seeks to create a balance between the different literary genres and theological hermeneutics. Ricoeur's method of intertextual interpretation is not without criticism from those who hold to a more authoritative rendering of interpretation from the biblical texts.

> Ricoeur's critics (like Hans Frei) have long wondered if his intertextualism is not a notion borrowed from poststructuralism that he imports into his exegesis rather than a determinative feature of the Bible discovered by a close reading of the texts themselves. Frei criticizes Ricoeur for using Continental theoretical notions such as "reader," "discourse," and "genre" in discussing

---

[2] Ibid., 41.

the Bible's diversity because the notions threaten to overwhelm the texts clear sense.[3]

Wallace notes that Ricoeur is careful to use general hermeneutical categories only insofar as they are dialectically related to exegetical practice, but not in control of that practice. Even though Ricoeur holds to this premise, Frei continues to question his methods, asking whether Ricoeur is actually a voice for the Christian community when he exposes the differences rather than thematic unity of the Bible. The consistent criticism of Ricoeur by Frei is that his literary-critical hermeneutic emphasizes the Bible's conflicts in genre and style at the expense of the clearly established stories found within the texts.

"As did Barth, Frei argues that the Bible is best construed as a sustained story unified by the character of Jesus in the Gospels, and that a literal or realistic reading…best renders the objective identity of Jesus by keeping the story free from corrosive influence of the reader's subjective impressions in determining the story's meaning."[4]

> The aim of an exegesis which simply looks for the sense of a story (but does not identify sense with religious significance for the reader) is in the final analysis that of reading the story itself. We ask if we agree on what we find there, and we discover its patterns one to another. And therefore the theoretical devices we use to make our reading more alert, appropriate, and intelligent ought to be designed to leave the story itself as unencumbered as possible.[5]

Frei purports to offer a more pure rendering of the text as he supports an interpretive strategy that allows for the text's own meaning. In other words, the reader does not place onto

---

[3] Ibid., 42.

[4] Ibid., 41.

[5] Hans Frei, *The Identity of Jesus Christ,* (Eugene, OR: Wipf and Stock Publishers, 1998).

the text his or her own meaning, which tends to impact and influence the text giving it a different meaning than what it "means to say itself." Thus, one possible weakness in Ricoeur's hermeneutic approach is that placing certain expectations on the text through intertextual interpretation manipulates the meaning of the story, creating some disassociation between the text and the reader. In addition, it creates a discrepancy between what the reader thinks the text means or should mean and what it actually does mean.

In analyzing Wallace's discussion of the use of theological-literary interpretation, he has provided some illuminating thoughts on Ricoeur's use of this method and its role in the varying categories of narrative approaches. He has also raised some important issues that continue to be developed concerning the use of narrative hermeneutics.

One of the issues implied within Wallace's discussion is that of intertextualism versus intratextualism. Hans Frei is a major proponent of intratextual interpretation (strict adherence to the text). Wallace has pointed out the criticism received by Ricoeur due to his intertextual interpretive approach. When such questions are asked of a text such as genre, syntax, style, and subject matter, the reader may impose his or her own meaning onto the text. I support Wallace's critique of Ricoeur concerning the use of intertextual hermeneutics; however, I see some benefits to asking certain questions of the text (syntax, grammar, socio-historical setting) as long as the autonomy of the text is not hindered.

Wallace's overall intent is to explain the hermeneutics of Frei and Ricoeur in terms of a synthesis/cooperation of the two. However, there are some stated weaknesses to Ricoeur's approach, particularly in his willingness to challenge the Biblical text through emphasizing literary conflicts in style and genre at the expense of its unified depictions of Jesus in the Gospels. The counter-criticism that I have, in all fairness, is that Wallace failed to expose any weaknesses that may exist regarding Frei's hermeneutic approach. While Wallace did provide a particularly illuminating discussion on Frei's critique of Ricoeur, there was no consideration given to the possible criticism of Frei.

One issue that could have been raised is the issue of a literal reading of the Biblical text that is supported by Frei. While one basis of my thesis is to emphasize the effectiveness of intratextualism, (which Frei also affirms), I do not necessarily find all of Frei's arguments to be superior to other forms of exegesis. Wallace makes reference to the idea of a "literal" reading of the Biblical text and how Frei affirms that this means of exegesis prevents a disassociation between the reader and the text. However, a literal reading alone is not always sufficient in capturing the depth and meaning of a text. One must inevitably resort to some literary analysis or even an epexegesis (deeper interpretation) in order to arrive at a proper understanding of the text.

Overall, I found Wallace's discussion very helpful in exposing the fact that there are various methods of narrative discourse and there is no single means by which a narrative interpretation is employed. The overwhelming issue in debate lies between the categories of general and specific hermeneutics.

Meaning as Reference

Hans Frei offers discourse on the historical development of narrative interpretation within the context of English and German theology. Due to the rise of controversy between two groups, Pietists and Supernaturalists, there was much debate concerning rationalistic and historical-critical interpretation of the Bible. This debate created discussions concerning the meaning of Biblical texts and the ways in which the meaning is referenced. Frei expounds on two categories of reference: historical or ostensive reference, and ideal reference.

Frei presents the discussion on ostensive reference by providing somewhat of a historical background of its origin. The supernaturalist group polemically discussed what they felt ought to be the specific nature of the inspiration of scripture, which is the literal truth of scripture. The pietist and orthodox persuasions differed from the supernaturalists in that they still used scriptural inspiration as an automatic warrant for claims on behalf of the text.

> In contrast to the orthodox and the pietists, the supernaturalists had to meet rationalistic and historical-critical interpretations of the Bible on the latter's home ground...It is a far cry from the earlier identification of explicative meaning with historical judgment, for which the fulfillment of prophecy was a function of the providentially ordered literal or figural harmony of earlier with later biblical narratives, a scheme that was at once literary and historical...The focus from both ends of the spectrum was increasingly on the identity of explicative meaning with the historical or ostensive reference of the texts.[6]

German theologian, S. J. Baumgarten (1706–1757) was an instrumental figure who argued that even the words of scripture or the forms in which the books of the Bible were written were inspired by God during the times of the German Enlightenment. "Baumgarten tended to distinguish sharply between the words and the subject matter of the Bible and to equate the latter much more than the former with revelation. To that extent his argument for the uniqueness and truth of the Bible was really a plea in behalf of a special, positive revelation."[7]

Frei focuses on Baumgarten because his ideas tend to resonate with what Baumgarten tried to argue concerning biblical narrative. "Baumgarten defended the credibility of the referent or subject matter of the Bible, the biblical story, against those who questioned it on philosophical or religious as well as factual grounds."[8] I make the above reference on the basis that

---

[6] Hans Frei, *The Eclipse of Biblical Narrative,* (New Haven: Yale University Press, 1974) 87.

[7] Ibid., 89.

[8] Ibid., 89.

Frei also defends the credibility of biblical subject matter, vis-à-vis those who hold greater loyalty to philosophical critique of scripture, rather than yielding to the authority of scripture. This has been one of the fundamental arguments concerning the methodological comparisons of Frei and Ricoeur.

Baumgarten further affirms that the historical referent, or the factual history, which claims to be revelation, is the governing principle for the explicative sense of the texts. They make sense to the extent that they can be shown to refer to these events faithfully.

> Hermeneutics is clearly on its way toward a notion of explicative interpretation in which a biblical narrative makes sense in accordance with its author's intention and the culture he exemplifies. And the meaning of the narrative is the subject matter to which the words refer. For Baumgarten, as for other conservatives or Supernaturalists, the subject matter of the words is the revelation that forms the content of the Bible.[9]

Frei notes that Baumgarten belongs to a transitional period around the middle eighteenth century in which German historical criticism and general hermeneutics began to emerge. The issue in debate between the supernaturalist group and the older conservatives was the issue of the unity of the Bible. Supernaturalists argued scriptural unity from the fulfillment of prophecy as a historical fact and not upon the basis of a single divine authorship—a single sense of the text that could be interpreted typologically.

"The case for the logical distinction but factual convergence between historical judgment and explicative hermeneutics was obviously very strong when even conservative theological views moved away from theories of direct divine inspiration of

---

[9] Ibid., 91.

the words, beginning instead to defend the factuality of the revealed reports."[10]

The nature of narrative hermeneutics is such that much of the Bible covers a continuous chronological sequence, which creates the effect of being a single story. The context of meaning as reference is such that whatever happened in the story established the meaning of the narrative texts. Frei informs that the alliance of historical-critical method with hermeneutics was a bit much for some. At the close of the eighteenth century and the beginning of the nineteenth century, a small protest erupted from the conservative rationalist camp.

Frei points out one such thinker within the conservative rationalist circle, Carl Friedrich Stäudlin of Göttingen. Stäudlin claimed that many of the proponents of historical-critical procedure falsely claimed that it provided an exhaustive explicative interpretation of the texts. Historical-critical exegesis exemplified a large scholarly movement, which Stäudlin and others were not completely opposed to. This movement created a convergence of the meaning of biblical narratives with the shape of the events to which they refer.

Frei introduces another movement during the eighteenth century concerning meaning as ideal reference. This philosophical tradition was headed by Christian Wolff. Wolff was a student of Leibniz as well as John Locke.

> In the description of concepts Wolff makes the moves that have the most important hermeneutic consequences. He distinguishes two kinds of conceptual definition or explanation. (He translated the Latin term *definitio* by the German *Erklarung,* one of the few technical usages in which he was not to be followed by the general tradition of German philosophical vocabulary.)[11]

---

[10] Ibid., 92.
[11] Ibid., 97.

The two concepts that Wolff asserts are the nominal definition or verbal explanation and the reality definition. The nominal or verbal explanation (which Wolff calls *definitio nominalis, Worterklarung)*, involves the statement of the concept and its distinguishing characteristics. The reality definition or subject matter explanation *(definitio realis, Sacherklarung)* is concerned with the ultimate explanatory basis of something signified by the concept. Reality definition can be thought of as either demonstration or experience. Wolff provides practical examples of each conceptual definition. Worterklarung: "the definition of a clock by its function; a machine for indicating the hours." Sacherklarung: "explanation of a clock by its component parts rather than its function."[12]

The nature of meaning as ideal reference is such that words properly used refer. Words signify or name possible things, which have an ideal status in which they are known by way of the mind's apprehension of their actuality through the senses. Hans Frei has provided the development of meaning-as-reference as he expounds on the conservative movement of the eighteenth century in German theology. His approach differs considerably from that of Paul Ricoeur, as Ricoeur discusses metaphor as reference in the following section.

Metaphor as Reference

The purpose of this section is to provide an analysis of Ricoeur's account of reference in contrast to that of Hans Frei. The major objective here is to explore Ricoeur's understanding and use of reference in such a way that his methods may be recognized in light of what we have seen thus far throughout the thesis. Both Frei and Ricoeur have distinct hermeneutic styles that should begin to be evident at this point. Frei discussed reference from the perspective of *meaning,* while I will show that Ricoeur's approach to reference involves *metaphor.*

---

[12] Ibid., 97.

James Fodor offers insight into Ricoeur's use of metaphorical reference in his book *Christian Hermeneutics: Paul Ricoeur and the Refiguring of Theology.*[13]

Fodor first asserts that Ricoeur's thesis is that all discourse bears the distinctive characteristic of making a reference to reality. Ricoeur's thesis is developed in light of anti-reference biases that appear in certain forms of contemporary literary criticism in which there is a desire to distinguish ordinary, nonpoetic discourse from poetic language along the lines of their distinctive referential modalities. According to Ricoeur, these literary critics focus on three main principles:

> First, poetic language is said to present a certain fusion between meaning and sense and the senses. Secondly, in contrast to ordinary language (with its thoroughly referential character), poetic language tends to produce an object closed in on itself. Thirdly, because of this centripetal nature of poetic language, only a fictional experience or an experience of virtual life can be articulated.[14]

Fodor wants to shed light on why Ricoeur intently defends poetic language and metaphor against the above charges as well as the criticism that it is merely emotive and noncognitive. Ricoeur maintains two reasons for his defense of poetic (metaphorical) discourse. One evolves out of the tradition of philosophy, while the other specifically relates to the biblical text.

In the first case, Fodor points out that in the history of Western thought, the assumption has been that poetic texts are in some sense deviant. In other words, poetic texts are scrutinized, regarded as unacceptable, and perceived as not having real truth value. They are regarded as mere expressions of subjective emotions by more harsh critics. This view

---

[13] James Fodor, *Christian Hermeneutics: Paul Ricoeur and the Refiguring of Theology*, (New York: Clarendon Press Oxford, 1995).
[14] Ibid., 147.

originates from what is called logical positivism. "The positivist criticism of religion claimed either that sentences about God were meaningless (since the noun had no reference, predicates could neither be applied nor withheld) or simply emotive expressions without any cognitive value."[15] It is Ricoeur's primary objective to combat and challenge this positivist view. Interestingly, this bias was not only confined to one genre of text, but also included literary criticism, moral reflection, theology, and aesthetics, according to Fodor.

The second reason that Ricoeur defends poetic texts is found within his own theology concerning the status of the Christian scriptures. Fodor affirms that Ricoeur characterizes the Bible as a "poem" in a broad, technical sense. Ricoeur argues that this technical sense of poetics includes the totality of literary genres that function differently than ordinary language, especially scientific discourse (which positivists oppose).

> In this technical sense, poetics includes the totality of literary genres, and its distinctiveness resides in the manner in which these genres exercise a referential function that differs from the descriptive referential function of ordinary language and above all of scientific discourse. Any discourse, therefore, which is not characterized by straightforward reference to a particular thing, situation, or event would seem to be an instance of poetic discourse. Descriptive scientific discourse, as its polar opposite, would be characterized by what Ricoeur calls first-order reference: either direct reference to the familiar objects of perception or indirect reference to physical entities that science reconstructs as underlying the objects of perception.[16]

---

[15] Ibid., 150.
[16] Ibid., 151.

This first-order reference is approached from a phenomenological perspective; however, Ricoeur has incorporated it into his hermeneutic approach as well. "First order reference is what is made, for the most part, in ordinary language. In the case of poetic texts, however, the reference is not to the world in any ordinary sense, but to something analogous to the world, something deeper and more fundamental."[17]

Ricoeur builds from the first-order reference and introduces a second-order reference. The second-order reference is developed in light of the task of hermeneutics to explicate on the *world* where first-order reference does not. The first-order reference presupposes a *suspension* of literal meaning due to its reference to an analogous world, thus creating the need for a second-level denotation to be attained. What Ricoeur attempts to achieve through the use of a second-order is a theory or hermeneutic approach of reference, which accounts for those literary genres that lack a referential function altogether. Ricoeur argues that truth claims are not confined to scientific or logical discourse but are also made in poetical and metaphorical discourse as well. Ricoeur's approach logically counteracts and capitalizes on the positivist views and the critics of poetic texts.

Ricoeur holds that metaphor does not replace first-order reference with a second-order reference, but rather, it transforms literal reference altogether.

> Poetic language also speaks of reality, but it does so at another level than does scientific language. It does not show us a world already there, as does descriptive or didactic language but...another level of reality...It is an eclipsing of the objective manipulable world, an illuminating of the life-world, of non-manipulable being-in-the-world, which seems to me to be the

---

[17] Ibid., 153.

fundamental   ontological   import   of   poetic language.[18]

Ricoeur's methods can be credited to Husserl based on the phenomenological methods used to present his arguments on metaphor. I will provide discourse on Ricoeur's analysis of Husserl's phenomenology in the following chapter. However, it is important to note that Ricoeur's notion of suspension is one adopted from Husserl, but Ricoeur modifies and transposes it into his own theory of reference.

> Although Ricoeur is primarily indebted to Husserl for the use of the phenomenological method in general, he nevertheless employs the term (suspension or *epoche*), in some instances at least, in markedly different ways from Husserl. Whereas for Husserl *epoche* signifies a methodological attitude, a bracketing or suspension of belief in the natural world for methodological gain, Ricoeur quite often uses the term to point out an essential capacity within language itself to founder or subvert itself.[19]

In addition to crediting Husserl for his formative thesis, Ricoeur also shares a similar ethos with Kant (which will also be discussed more in-depth later).

> Both Kant and Ricoeur hold that productive imagination is a schematizing function. But whereas Kant understood such schematism as joining empirical and intelligible aspects of the concept, Ricoeur gives the notion of schema a linguistic   twist: productive   imagination schematizes metaphoric attribution. What Ricoeur does, then, is transpose this Kantian insight into his

---

[18] Ibid., 154.
[19] Ibid., 155.

> own theory of metaphor by accommodating it to fit
> a semantic or verbal analysis.[20]

I note Ricoeur's relation to Husserl and Kant as it provides some insight into their influences on his hermeneutic approach in comparison to that of Frei. As I close this section, I want to provide an assessment of the findings thus far regarding the hermeneutic approaches of Frei and Ricoeur as relates to reference.

It is important to note that Frei and Ricoeur both argue reference in light of some opposing issues. Frei exposed the debate between the Pietists and Supernaturalists during the eighteenth century as he presented a case for historical-critical method in which he proposed two areas of interest: ostensive and ideal reference to explicate on the *meaning* of texts as reference. The debate between the Pietists and Supernaturalists arose out of the quagmire of German theological conservatism during the latter part of the eighteenth century and the beginning of the nineteenth century.

Ricoeur argues the use of *metaphor* as reference due to his affinity toward the use of poetic language and his view of the Bible as a "poem." His hermeneutics espouses a dual approach to metaphoric language as he argues in light of certain positivist views against poetic and many other forms of literary genres of Western thought. Ricoeur introduces the uses of first- and second-order reference to explicate on metaphor as reference.

The contrasting elements of their methodologies exist in their commitments to general (Ricoeur) and specific (Frei) hermeneutics. This is the continuing theme that runs throughout the thesis. However, I do not wish to make this statement frivolously or unsubstantiated. The hermeneutics of both Frei and Ricoeur have been heavily shaped by theologians and philosophers whose ideas resonate respectively. It is an important factor to note that Frei has been influenced by Barth as both share similar hermeneutic approaches, especially in the area of Biblical authority. Ricoeur has been influenced by such

---

[20] Ibid., 160.

philosophers as Husserl and Kant, thus sharing a similar ethos concerning literary critique of biblical texts and employing more use of phenomenological and existential methods to narrative.

The next chapter will illuminate and expound on these contrasting characteristics of Frei and Ricoeur and will provide some important points of convergence and divergence between the two.

Part III

Philosophical Uses

Frei and Ricoeur: Prolegomena vs. Phenomenology

Narrative hermeneutics has many uses and categories through which a theologian or "narratologist" might engage a biblical text. In this section, I will offer discourse on some philosophical aspects of narrative from the perspectives of Frei and Ricoeur. Of the various types of narrative theologies, I will concentrate on two: fundamental and phenomenological. I chose these two types in particular because one is theological and the other existential.

There is a conflict of interest concerning philosophical idealism within the framework of theology according to Frei. However, Ricoeur proposes that there can be interdependence between the two and moreover, one cannot function without the other; there is a phenomenological presupposition of hermeneutics and a hermeneutic presupposition of phenomenology.

Is there a place for philosophically based hermeneutics in theology? Is one method more or less effective in the task of articulating God's grace through the person and salvific event of Jesus Christ? It will be my task to engage these questions further and to assess the positions of Frei and Ricoeur concerning the philosophical uses of narrative hermeneutics in theology.

Prolegomena

Hans Frei discusses five types of theology in which the fourth type is provided by Karl Barth.[1] Barth calls his theology *prolegomena,* which represents a type of fundamental theology. For Barth, unlike Schleiermacher, fundamental theology (prolegomena) is part of dogmatics and is not a procedure for correlating theology to other disciplines. The central idea advanced by Barth is that theology, as a function of the Church, is accountable to God for its discourse about God. The Church must be critical of any discourse about God as it represents the presence of God in light of obedience to God and his grace.

Barth maintains that the criterion of Christian discourse is Jesus Christ, who is the being of the Church. The question posed by Barth as a challenge to academic theology and other disciplines incorporated into theology is, does Christian discourse come from Jesus Christ, and move toward him, and is it in accordance with him? For Barth, theology is not philosophically grounded and is independent of any external description, whether metaphysically, philosophically, or scientifically. Also, theology as a systematic procedure is not a set of universal, formal criteria that are certain and all-encompassing, stated apart from a context of specific application. "But it obviously seems to him that such rules, even as formal as this, must be ad hoc. It must depend on the specific context in which one speaks; it cannot be context-invariant."[2] Distinctions should be made according to and depending upon the issue at hand regarding theological discourse.

> "Theology as specific and critical Christian self-description and self-examination by the Church of its language takes absolute priority over

---

[1] Points taken from his book, Hans Frei, *Types of Christian Theology,* (New Haven: Yale University Press, 1992).

[2] Ibid., 40. This idea is advanced from Barth's discussion on first and second-order discourse or theology. Barth wants to make the point that certain formal uses of discourse about Christianity are not beyond his scope of use. He affirms that they must however, be ad hoc or specific to a certain context.

theology as an academic discipline. Philosophy as conceptual system describing and referring to reality is not a basis on which to build theology, and even philosophy as a set of formal, universal rules or criteria for what may count as coherent and true in Christian discourse as in every other kind of conceptual practice is not basic to or foundational of Christian theology."[3]

Does Barth claim that there are no instances when formal rules or criteria for coherence may be applied to theological discourse? No, in fact, he maintains that one cannot use human language without some formal guidance. Barth also affirms that we cannot function without such formal categories and distinctions as those between meaning and truth, sense and reference, description and explanation. Here Barth acknowledges the need for formal rules and criteria, however, those rules must strictly adhere to (and be governed by) whatever specific theological issue is at hand.

Absolute priority must be given to Christian theology as self-description for the Christian community. "Barth acknowledges the need for a formal or technical philosophical vocabulary in theology. If theology in that criteriological sense can be firmly governed by theology, one need not fear a second use or understanding of philosophy within theology."[4] In other words, certain checks and balances must apply to any external understanding of theology, and as long as any such formal discussion fits into a proper perspective, it is an acceptable application of thought. The use of philosophy must be subordinate to theology if used to explicate or discuss Christian theology.

Frei, like Barth, holds to a similar conviction, as we have seen throughout the contrasting elements between him and Ricoeur. Neither Barth nor Frei would totally exclude

---

[3] Ibid., 40.
[4] Ibid., 41.

philosophy from theology as long as it is subordinate to theology.

> Barth finds the heart of theological discourse in the constant transition between first-order Christian statements, especially biblical confession and exegesis, and their second-order redescription, in which description as internal dogmatic description makes use of third-order free, unsystematic, and constant reference to conceptual patterns of a non-Christian, nontheological kind — including phenomenology, conceptual analysis, Hegelian philosophy, analyses of contemporary culture, and so on.[5]

Barth here is in contrast to such thinkers as David Tracy, for whom the meaning of Christian statements is their anthropological or experiential reference. "The text means what it says, and so the reader's redescription is just that, a redescription and not the discovery of the text as symbolic representation of something else more profound."[6]

Barth goes on to say, however, that during this process of redescription, one will inevitably employ his or her own experiences and thoughts in order to correlate them with the task of redescription. This process of redescription is governed by what Barth calls appropriateness to the subject matter. In other words, the criterion of the process is governed by the context and not imposed upon it. He claims that for theology there does not exist any context-invariant criteriology.

> Barth affirms that the final result is that prolegomena is part of dogmatics itself; it attempts insofar as possible — and it is a limited matter indeed — to exhibit the rules or fragments of rules implicit in the ruled use of language which is the sign system of the sociolinguistic

---

[5] Ibid., 43.
[6] Ibid., 44.

community called the Church...The relationship between internal self-description and external description thus remains ad hoc, with freedom for each side, possible family resemblance, and obedience to the criterion of the priority of Christian self-description as the task of the Church.[7]

Frei claims that Barth has come as close as anybody in his generation to discovering and developing a specific mode of studying scripture in which external and internal Christian description converge. "Literary study of a certain kind of biblical narrative is a distinct mode that may or may not overlap with historical study, and it bears a strong family resemblance to theological exegesis, especially the kind employing the literal sense."[8]

In the final analysis, as stated earlier, Barth claims that the relationship between internal self-description and external description remains ad hoc (specific to the issue at hand) with some autonomy given to each kind of reference. The highest priority must remain with Christian self-description, as it is the task of the Church. Frei does not intend to show that Barth's theology is "anti-philosophical" in its discourse. Frei does want to make the distinction that any external description of the Christian faith should be critiqued in such a way that it does not impose any meaning onto the biblical text and that the biblical text remain autonomous throughout any exegesis.

Barth does, however, challenge any "universality" of meaning regarding Christian redescription. For Barth, the proper method of referring to a text is through an ad hoc or context variant criteriology.

---

[7] Ibid., 46.
[8] Ibid., 46.

Phenomenology

As Frei tends to gravitate toward the Barthian idea of prolegomena, Ricoeur holds to a Husserlian idealism, which posits a phenomenological presupposition of hermeneutics. Ricoeur presents an argument in favor of some various ways in which philosophy can be pursued regarding hermeneutics. Ricoeur proposes two theses in his discussion of phenomenology[9]: the first thesis proposes that there is a dichotomous relationship between hermeneutics and phenomenology, which will be discussed within the context of the phenomenological ideas of Husserl. The second thesis involves the possibility of a convergence or mutual existence between hermeneutics and phenomenology. Ricoeur proposes that neither can be constituted without a presupposition of the other. Phenomenology is presupposed by hermeneutics as much as hermeneutics is presupposed by phenomenology.

Ricoeur introduces the idealism of Husserl as it is submitted to the critique of hermeneutics. Ricoeur provides a schematic discussion in which Husserl's idealism is expressed within five modes of discourse:

(a)   The first discussion begins from a polemic position of phenomenology in which it is characterized as a *combatant philosophy*. This means that it will always be in opposition to another view. Husserl asserts that this polemical style of philosophy claims a *radicality* or radical nature, which he calls *aus letzter Begründung* [ultimate grounding].

"That does not mean there have not been several ways answering to this unique idea; the idea of foundation is rather that which secures the equivalence and convergence of the ways

---

[9] Paul Ricoeur, *Hermeneutics and the Human Sciences,* (New York: Cambridge University Press, 1981). See also Ricoeur's work on Husserl in his book, *Husserl: An Analysis of His Phenomenology,* (Evanston: Northwestern University Press, 1967).

(logical, Cartesian, psychological, historico-teleological, etc.). There are real beginnings or rather paths towards a beginning, elicited by the absolute absence of presuppositions. It is thus fruitless to inquire into the motivation for such a radical beginning; there is no reason internal to a domain for raising the question of origin."[10]

(b)   The second discussion involves the concept of an *Erfahrungsfeld* [field of experience]. The idea behind this concept is that the principle of intuition is the field and the first truth is an experience. Husserl affirms that phenomenology is concerned with natural experience and is not situated in another world.

(c)   The third principle concerns plenary intuition as subjectivity; all transcendence is doubtful because it is advanced by *Abschattungen* [sketches or profiles], while immanence is not doubtful because it is not advanced by anything presumptive.

Husserl claims that all transcendence is doubtful based upon the following patterns of reasoning: "Because the convergence of these *Abschattungen* is always presumptive; the presumption can be disappointed by some discordance; consciousness can form the hyperbolic hypothesis of a radical discordance of appearances, which is the very hypothesis of the destruction of the world."[11]

(d)   The fourth mode involves a more engaging discussion of transcendental phenomenology. Husserl asserts that there exists a parallel between phenomenology and psychology, thus leading to some confusion of the two disciplines (one being transcendental and the other empirical). The difference consists not in descriptive features but in ontological indices called *Seinsgeltung*

---

[10] Ibid., 103.
[11] Ibid., 103.

[validity of being]. Husserl's argument suggests that it is only through the loss of psychological realism that the world can be revealed as "pregiven," the body as "existing," and nature as "being."

(e)   The fifth mode involves ethical reflection expressed as *aus letzter Selbstverantwortung* [ultimate self-responsibility]. "The philosophical conversion is the supremely autonomous act. What we have called the ethical nuance is thus immediately implied in the foundational act, insofar as the latter can only be self-positing. It is in this sense that it is ultimately self-responsible."[12]

I will briefly provide the opposing positions of hermeneutics vis-à-vis the Husserlian ideal of phenomenology as Ricoeur maintains that the antithetical approach facilitates the establishment of dialogue between the two. I will provide the critical response to Husserl's idealism followed by Ricoeur's discourse on the convergence of hermeneutics and phenomenology.

(a)   The first question placed upon Husserlian idealism by hermeneutics concerns intentionality, which is weakened by the concept of *subject-object relation.* Ricoeur points out that the subject-object relation creates a need to search for something that unifies the meaning of the object, consequently being founded subjectively.

(b)   Husserl's discourse on intuition is challenged by the hermeneutic necessity for all understanding to be governed and mediated by an interpretation.

"The dependence of interpretation on understanding explains why explication always precedes reflection and comes before any constitution of the object by a sovereign subject."[13]

---

[12] Ibid., 105.
[13] Ibid., 107.

Intention, situation and original addressee constitute the *Sitz-im-Leben* [site-in-life] of the text. The possibility of multiple interpretations is opened up by the text, which is thus freed from its *Sitz-im-Leben*. Beyond the polysemy of words in a conversation is the polysemy of a text, which invites multiple readings. This is the moment of interpretation in the technical sense of *textual exegesis*.[14]

(c)   The third critique of Husserlian idealism finds problematic the idea that the place of ultimate foundation is subjectivity and that all transcendence is doubtful and only immanence is indubitable. Ricoeur states that "only a hermeneutics of communication can assume the task of incorporating the critique of ideology into self-understanding"[15] Ricoeur affirms that hermeneutics can account for both the character of the ideological phenomenon, and the possibility of beginning. "Hermeneutics can do this because, in contrast to phenomenological idealism, the subject of which it speaks is always open to the efficacy of history. Textual exegesis and critique of ideology are the two privileged routes along which understanding is developed into interpretation."[16]

(d)   The fourth hermeneutic affirmation suggests that the hermeneutical task is to discern the matter of the text rather than the psychology of the author.

A radical way of placing the primacy of subjectivity in question is to take the theory of the text as the hermeneutical axis. Insofar as the meaning of the text is rendered autonomous with respect to the subjective intention of its author,

---

[14] Ibid., 108.
[15] Ibid., 110.
[16] Ibid., 111.

the essential question is not to recover, behind the text, the lost intention, but to unfold, in front of the text, the world which it opens up and discloses.[17]

(e)   The final opposition to Husserlian idealism concerns the ultimate self-responsibility of the mediating subject. The task of hermeneutics, here, is to make the subject the final category of understanding as opposed to the first. It does not purport or impose any meaning of the text, but rather it responds to the matter of the text. Ricoeur calls this understanding *distanciation*, which implements all the strategies of suspicion, in which the critique of ideology is a principal modality. "Distanciation, in all its forms and figures, constitutes the critical moment in understanding."[18]

Ricoeur's critical analysis and response to Husserlian idealism provides the opportunity for a development of what he calls *hermeneutic phenomenology*. Ricoeur is careful to state that he seeks only to show the possibility of this hermeneutic phenomenology and not to work it out.

It seeks only to show its possibility by establishing, on the one hand, that beyond the critique of Husserlian idealism, phenomenology remains the unsurpassable presupposition of hermeneutics; and on the other hand, that phenomenology cannot carry out its program of constitution without constituting itself in the interpretation of the experience of the ego.[19]

Ricoeur points to four phenomenological presuppositions of hermeneutics.

---

[17] Ibid., 111.
[18] Ibid., 113.
[19] Ibid., 114.

(a)   He claims that the most basic and fundamental presupposition is that every question concerning *etant* [being] is a question about the meaning of that being. For Ricoeur, the ontological question is a phenomenological question. It is thus a hermeneutic issue due to the meaning being concealed by everything forbidding access to it. Due to the issue or question of meaning, there exists a phenomenological status which must be recognized.

(b)   Ricoeur proposes that hermeneutics also relates to phenomenology through its recourse to *distanciation*. "Hermeneutic distanciation is not unrelated to the phenomenological *epoché*, which is interpreted in a non-idealist sense as an aspect of the intentional movement of consciousness towards meaning. For all consciousness of meaning involves a moment of distanction."[20]

(c)   The third aspect that hermeneutics shares with phenomenology concerns linguistic meaning. Ricoeur notes Gadamer for his thesis on this subject in which he discusses the secondary character of the problematic of language. Hermeneutic philosophy begins with the experience of art, which is not necessarily linguistic. According to Ricoeur, the most important phenomenological presupposition of hermeneutics is constituted by the reference of the linguistic order back to the structure of experience (which comes to language).

(d)   The fourth and final assessment of phenomenological presuppositions of hermeneutics involves the development of perceptual experience in cooperation with the hermeneutics of historical experience. Husserl began to develop a new model of truth elicited from the

---

[20] Ibid., 116.

phenomenology of perception, which entered into the domain of the historical-hermeneutic sciences.

It is well known how, on the one hand, Husserl continued to develop the properly temporal implications of perceptual experience. He was thus led, by his own analyses, towards the historicity of human experience as a whole. In particular, it became increasingly evident that the presumptive, inadequate, unfinished character which perceptual experience acquires from its temporal structure could be applied step by step to the whole of historical experience.[21]

Ricoeur has maintained throughout his analysis that there must be a cooperative relationship between phenomenology and hermeneutics and that one presupposes the other, but that one does not function without the other. "An interdependence and a complimentarity must be established between the regulative norms of true knowledge and the constitutive operations of free action."[22]

In conclusion, Frei and Ricoeur converge on the point that there can be some common ground between theology and philosophy and that there is even some imbrication within their functions respectively. For Frei, however, theology is not philosophically grounded and is able to stand independent of any external description. Frei's critique is most concerned with responding to academic theology as he contends that it does not provide the best account of Christian discourse about God. It is here that the major point of divergence exists. In contrast to Frei, Ricoeur proposes that there is a phenomenological presupposition of hermeneutics or that there is a mutually dependent existence between the two.

---

[21] Ibid., 119.

[22] Paul Ricoeur, *The Conflict of Interpretations: Essays in Hermeneutics*, (Evanston: Northwestern Press, 1974) 213.

In order to properly engage in Christian hermeneutics, the highest priority must be given to Christian self-description as the criterion of Christian discourse is Jesus Christ. This does not mean that no usages of philosophical ideas may be used to provide discourse about God. However, phenomenological and philosophical disciplines must be subordinate to Christian discourse and not used in subversion to it.

Part IV

Practical Uses

Frei and Ricoeur: Narrative and Practical Theology

In this last section I want to provide some discussion on the practical aspects of narrative hermeneutics from the perspectives of Frei and Ricoeur. As we have looked at the theological, theoretical, and philosophical uses, practical discourse will add a well-rounded dimension to what has been revealed. I think it to be a worthy endeavor to assess the practical aspects of narrative hermeneutics and to see how certain positions function if taken seriously in actual practice.

I will discuss three areas of interest concerning practical theology and narrative: pastoral praxeology, textual autonomy, and expository interpretation of scripture. In light of the issues discussed concerning narrative theology, one would naturally want to know how stories may be preached. The question also arises as to the nature of how such hermeneutic principles apply to real life as opposed to referenced, how they are practiced rather than used philosophically, how they are taught rather than theorized.

Pastoral Praxeology

This assessment of pastoral praxeology as it relates to hermeneutics and *identity* will be an analysis of discourse provided by Ricoeur. Ricoeur argues that there are some dangers to be pointed out concerning hermeneutics. One danger is that of the possibility of hermeneutics becoming banal or commonplace. Ricoeur states that an academic hermeneutics would merely become one philosophy among many others and would not render any particularly illuminating discourse. It would create a certain redundancy because it would not arrive at any significant conclusion.

> It would become one rival philosophy occupying the same place as all others, the pretentious place of fundamental philosophy with, moreover, the vice of being a discourse about discourse, and therefore of being, I would say, redundant. This is the current peril facing hermeneutics to become this kind of discourse about discourse.[1]

Ricoeur argues that in the midst of the "self-complacency" of hermeneutics, the role of application is crucial and not merely a supplemental aspect of the interpretive process. In the basic process of hermeneutics, Ricoeur proposes that there must be understanding and explication, along with application. "Understanding and explication without application are not interpretation."[2] It is the recognition of application that combats this complacent, banal status of hermeneutics, which is important for pastoral ministry.

Ricoeur also wants to make the point that discourse is, in fact, an action. "I have the impression that this is taken for granted today and that we are no longer caught in the quarrel between praxis and discourse."[3] Ricoeur maintains that there are four main objects of interpretation: texts, events, institutions, and personages (personages meaning characters or roles of persons). These objects are all interrelated, and hermeneutics takes place when these events are interpreted.

Another problem pointed out by Ricoeur is that of *identity.* "It seems to me that this is also a problem for those concerned with pastoral ministry inasmuch as there is always the problem

---

[1] Paul Ricoeur, *Figuring the Sacred,* (Minneapolis: Augsburg Fortress Press, 1995) 304.
[2] Ibid., 304.
[3] Ibid., 305.

of the *who*."[4] The questions arise as to who is the actor? Who is being acted upon? Who relates to whom? Ricoeur asserts that the issue of identity can be discussed in the form of narrative unity of a life. This narrative unity of a life maintains that the identity of an actor and the objects/ subjects of his or her intervention consist in a unity. In other words, through the incorporation of the elements of identity, events, and object/subjects, a plot is formed within the narrative creating "narrative unity" in regards to the question of who.

Textual Autonomy

Hans Frei proposes a different hermeneutic than Ricoeur as he does not concentrate on the problem of identity but rather the issue of textual autonomy. Frei espouses a hermeneutic with a few notable characteristics:

> (1) The autonomy of the text as a self-sufficient, non-referential organism; (2) the location of meaning in the work itself quite apart from the authorial intention or reader-response; (3) the inseparability of form and content; (4) an insistence on intrinsic criticism and the concomitant sanctions against the heresy of paraphrase and (5) the necessity of self-surrender to and participation in the experiential knowledge obtained through the text.[5]

As James Fodor proposes, Frei's most critical claim concerning textual autonomy is that a text's sense of meaning is independent of its reception.[6] The meanings of narratives are autonomous with regard to the beliefs, convictions, and attitudes of their readers or recipients.

---

[4] Ibid., 306.
[5] Lynn Poland, *The New Criticism, Neoorthodoxy and the New Testament* (Chicago: Chicago Scholars Press, 1985) 120.
[6] James Fodor, *Christian Hermeneutics*, (New York: Oxford Press, 1995) 276.

The pivotal, and perhaps the most significant, argument in favor of textual autonomy is that the identity descriptions provided by the Gospels enable the reader to grasp the nature of the identity of Jesus Christ, regardless of whether or not the reader is a believer or nonbeliever. In other words, by allowing the text to speak for itself, the conclusions become clear and evident to the reader, eliminating much need for imposing any further meaning onto the text.

Fodor points out that Frei's attempt to interpret and extend Barth's defense of the sovereignty of the Word of God closely resembles a literary-critical strategy, which is uncharacteristic of Frei. "However tempting this interpretation may seem, it represents too facile a criticism, particularly in light of Frei's consistent refusal of all forms of relationism, that is, aligning theology to *any* kind of general philosophical or literary theory."[7] This point is important to note because Frei has maintained an opposing ideology to Ricoeur in this very domain. However, Frei does hold, to some extent, a philosophical view in regards to his hermeneutic approach.

> Philosophically Frei is dependent on P.F. Strawson's approach to reference and identity description, an approach which is essentially Russellian in shape. Following Bertrand Russell, Strawson distinguishes between demonstrative identification and descriptive identification. The former type of knowledge is immediate and direct while the latter is indirect and mediated...It is possible for any subject to have a fully coherent idea of a particular object given under a description-based identity description such as that offered by Frei of Jesus, namely, Jesus of Nazareth is the Savior who underwent

---

[7] Ibid., 276.

all these things and who truly manifest as Jesus, the risen Christ.[8]

Fodor points out that both the believer and nonbeliever may acquire the identifying information about Jesus from the text but both may not take it at face value. One takes it as true and accurate, while the other considers it to be false and inaccurate. It is when a person actually believes and accepts that the Christian concepts are true that he or she will usually begin to live accordingly.

> The defining and salient feature of a realistic narrative resides not so much in its capacity to generate truth-claims, but in its rendering of an agent's identity, and through such rendering, to transform human beings. The emphasis in intratextualism is less on what texts *say* and more on what they are *used* for; less on theory and more on skill-based understanding and good practice; less on semantics, and more on pragmatics.[9]

Expository Interpretation of Scripture

In this last section I will discuss the uses of exposition and the hermeneutic implications of scriptural status, or rather, scriptural authority. One of the most critical controversies that has existed in Christian theology throughout the modern era is that of biblical interpretation. Due to the wide range and variety of interpretive methods, natural sciences, historical-critical methods, and other cultural traditions and religions, the subject of authority has been called into question.

Hans Frei has remained committed to biblical authority, even to the point of a stubborn refusal to be persuaded by other methods of discourse. Frei would support an expository method of scriptural interpretation due to its adherence to the text and

---

[8] Ibid., 277.
[9] Ibid., 279.

the means of "exposing" what already exists within the text. His is closely related to intratextuality, which Frei endorses consistently.

Before discussing exposition more in depth, I will provide some discussion on scriptural authority. Charles M. Wood argues that there are two opposing views in regards to scriptural authority. One view is liberal and the other conservative. Liberal hermeneutics posit that the texts should not be privileged on account of their supposed authority and that their authoritative status should have no bearing upon interpretation within a religious community.

Conservative hermeneutics posits that commitment to the authority of scripture is the proper way to understanding it. Conservatism holds that scrutinizing and testing a text and approaching it as any other material will cause one to miss the intended message. However, scriptural authority and expository interpretation is not necessarily exclusive to the conservative approach.

The most significant issue concerning this type of hermeneutic approach is the assessment of whether or not the status of authority has any bearing on the text's interpretation. Those views that oppose this status of authority maintain that the texts ought to be treated as informative resources. Charles Wood posits that any well-rounded account of scriptural authority will answer to three principal questions: (1) For what is this material authoritative? (2) How does it exercise its authority? (3) Why is it authoritative? "The first question concerns the scope of scripture's authority; the second, its character; and the third, its source. The same questions might be addressed by a descriptive account of scripture's authority for a community—an account of what is sometimes called de facto authority."[10] What then is the function of expository interpretation in light of scriptural authority?

---

[10] Garrett Green, *Scriptural Authority and Narrative Interpretation,* (Philadelphia: Fortress Press, 1987) 10.

"Expository preaching classically denotes any preaching that expounds scripture in a systematic way. It involves a careful analysis of a text's burden, grasping the point it makes, construing the text as a whole and discovering how its various themes relate to that central concern."[11] "The agenda for scripture's expository material is set by an interaction between the truth about God and the way God deals with people as a whole, on one hand, and the particular needs of specific contexts, on the other."[12]

James Rosscup provides four practical principles for the expositional method of hermeneutics.

1. Use the true text, God's Word, as closely as you can responsibly determine it by consulting specialists on textual criticism.

2. Employ the science of hermeneutics, with its interpretive principles.

3. Let these principles expose the meaning of a passage (i.e., do an exegetical study of the text) as a person follows prescribed rules in playing a game. Exegesis, then, is the application of hermeneutic principles to decide what a text says and means in its own historical, theological, contextual, literary, and cultural setting. The meaning thus obtained will be in agreement with other related scriptures.

4. Preach the exposition that flows from this process. Make conspicuous the true and essential original meaning and apply this meaning to present needs of hearers in their own cultural sitation.[13]

Rosscup argues that these key interpretive principles, when learned and developed through practice, provide substantial help

---

[11] John Goldingay, *Models for the Interpretation of Scripture*, (Grand Rapids, MI: Eerdmans Publishing Co., 1995) 266.
[12] Ibid., 271.
[13] John MacArthur, Jr. *Rediscovering Expository Preaching*, (Dallas: Word Publishing, 1992) 120.

in determining what God's Word says and means. The expositor can develop competence as an interpreter if he or she employs these important guidelines diligently, sanely, and competently. Furthermore, he or she can use these as a foundation for further developing hermeneutic skill.

I chose to discuss the expository method of interpretation because it is my own practical approach, as narrative is my own hermeneutic approach to doing theology (no bias intended). I will conclude this section with my own thoughts on the use of narrative hermeneutics along with an endorsement of expository interpretation.

I begin with a statement on the authority of scripture with which I concur, "Scripture is not authoritative when it is used 'in the cause of obscurantism, oppression, prejudice, racism, sexism, or anti-environmental purposes.'"[14] I believe that the narrative element of scripture provides a context out of which one may properly engage in a cogent, logical, and authoritative hermeneutic. James Barr further elaborates on this point in which he maintains that if attention is focused on the larger pattern of the biblical story that climaxes in the life, death, and resurrection of Christ, then "we shall have little doubt about the indispensability of the Bible to Christian faith and life."[15]

I am in favor of the narrative element of scripture because it provides an authoritative criterion upon which to base a passage of scripture. This criterion must be Christocentric (but not christomonistic, or Christ only) and must be in accordance with the character of Christ. Daniel Migliore provides three principles of interpreting scripture. First, scripture must be interpreted with literary and historical criticism or analysis. Second, it must be interpreted theocentrically; God's faithfulness in acts of judgment and mercy in the covenant with Israel and the person of Jesus Christ. Third, it must be

---

[14] Taken from Clark Williamson, Systematic Theology notes p. 57.
[15] Daniel Migliore, *Faith Seeking Understanding*, (Grand Rapids, MI: Eerdmans Publishing, 1991) 48.

interpreted contextually; practical engagement of the text with consideration of social and historical factors within.[16]

Scripture contains its own self-correcting hermeneutic, and scripture best interprets scripture. I conclude with a quote in which I also concur, "Inerrancy can be articulated in a more nuanced way, so as to argue that if we interpret the scripture responsibly and in the same way that it criticizes and interprets itself, it will not mislead us."[17]

---

[16] Ibid. Principles credited to Daniel Migliore, pp. 49–53.
[17] Clark Williamson, Systematic Theology notes, p. 58.

Conclusion

A few preliminary remarks are in order as I conclude the project of discussing the use of narrative hermeneutics. The appeal of narrative theology is such that it will be attractive to those concerned with reclaiming the centrality of scripture in modern theology. As I stated early on, the basis of this book is to compare the respective approaches of Hans Frei and Paul Ricoeur on some specific areas of interest. I have assessed the strengths and weaknesses of both, while explaining some various ways in which narrative theology is used.

Through the effective engagement of intratextual theology, which strictly adheres to the biblical text, I contend that the Christian story can best be articulated to the Christian community for the purpose of *believing* and not merely *knowing*. Both a believer and a nonbeliever can arrive at a level of understanding of the biblical text, but only the believer will attempt to live by it. Thus, I conclude that the major emphasis of theology (regardless of the method used) should be to convey an understanding of God that is life transforming, not merely an understanding that is informative and analytical.

I have undertaken this project by dividing the uses of narrative hermeneutics into four categories: theological, theoretical, philosophical, and practical. My intent here is to provide a well-rounded discussion of narrative hermeneutics that may account for a variety of considerations and conclusions.

My project has been twofold in nature: to endorse the use and method of intratextual interpretation and to provide discourse on two proponents of narrative hermeneutics (who have historically had opposing views)—Hans Frei and Paul Ricoeur. What constructive statements can be concluded overall concerning the methods of Frei and Ricoeur? What are the major points of divergence between the two that have been discussed? Are there any points of convergence that exist between Frei and Ricoeur to be considered? Finally, what are the strengths and weaknesses that have been exposed concerning the methodologies of Frei and Ricoeur concerning narrative theology?

One can conclude that some obvious differences exist between Frei and Ricoeur that are easily noted. It would be safe to say, on a lower level of analysis, that Frei is a "theologian" and Ricoeur is a "philosopher." Frei's methods proceed from the basis of the centrality of the Word of God and complete scriptural authority. Frei is a student of Barthian *Dogmatics* and thus argues in favor of a hermeneutic approach to scripture that does not align to or with secular, extra-biblical sources of information to be substantiated, legitimated, or interpreted. The theological framework for the authority of scripture is such that scripture is history-like, rather than like history for Frei. These characteristic are common methods of a theologian.

In contrast to Frei, Ricoeur proceeds from a philosophical, literary-critical method. Ricoeur is aligned with Edmund Husserl in that he maintains that the value of phenomenological method is crucial in the hermeneutic process. In fact, Ricoeur holds that there is a phenomenological presupposition of hermeneutics, and that there is no functioning of one without the other. Clearly, Ricoeur endorses the use of extra-biblical methods of interpretation, unlike Frei. Another significant characteristic of Ricoeur's hermeneutic approach is his relational understanding of general and specific hermeneutics. General hermeneutics refers to philosophy, while special hermeneutics refers to theology. The defining mark of Ricoeur's hermeneutic approach is his priority of the use of philosophy over theology, thus I call him a philosopher.

The major point of divergence between Frei and Ricoeur rests in the two methods of *intratextuality* and *intertextuality*. Frei espouses an intratextual hermeneutic, while Ricoeur maintains some referential notion to account for text-world relations. Frei criticizes Ricoeur's use of intertextual hermeneutics and posits that no recourse to reference is necessary.

Frei and Ricoeur converge on a number of issues, which I will note. Both Frei and Ricoeur obviously agree that narrative is an effective, if not ultimate, tool for understanding God's truth. Both emphasize the connections between biblical narratives and the formation of Christian identity. Neither argues nor bases Christian faith upon systematic apologetic methods. Both are willing to critique and correct the weaknesses and deficiencies that exist in their contrasting interpretive methods.

Now we come to the strengths and weaknesses of the methods of Frei and Ricoeur. In light of my thesis argument, that intratextual theology best illuminates and articulates Christian identity, I will base the strengths and weaknesses assessment of Frei and Ricoeur on this premise. Frei's narrative approach is such that in Christian theology, the story is the meaning of the doctrine, not the doctrine the meaning of the story. Frei's hermeneutic stance more closely adheres to my thesis in contrast to Ricoeur. Ricoeur holds to a philosophically based hermeneutic that does not necessarily reach the meaning of the biblical text, but rather critiques the text, and in a sense, tries to find the "meaning" of the meaning.

It is my contention that in light of articulating Christian identity, this is a possible point of weakness within Ricoeur's methodological approach. Frei's perception of Ricoeur is that he places higher priority on literary-critical reference and phenomenological presuppositions taking away from the text, thus creating a "watered down" interpretation (in light of Christian identity). However, Frei is inaccurate in this assumption of Ricoeur because Ricoeur would also insist that hearing the Gospel of Jesus Christ *is* the highest priority.

Frei presents a much stronger case, especially in his work *The Identity of Jesus Christ.* The basis of any hermeneutic approach should seek to interpret for the purpose of transforming and conforming the Christian community to the likeness and person of Christ. It should not seek, at least as the primary basis, to conform the biblical text to a particular community through the use of extra-biblical means of interpretation. I am opposed to this method because it tends to weaken the text, or rather, does not allow the power within the text to function properly. In other words, I argue in favor of textual autonomy, which allows the text to stand independent of interpretive strategies that impose meaning onto the text.

Ricoeur does, however, possess strengths in the area of asking questions of the text regarding genre, syntax, style, and subject matter. These questions are relevant and purposeful if one wants to gain a deeper understanding of a text. Ricoeur is strong in the area of literary criticism and provides a strong argument in favor of philological analysis. The grammar of a text should not be overlooked, as the meaning is found within the very grammar of a text. I see many benefits to asking certain questions of the text (syntax, grammar, socio-historical setting) as long as the autonomy of the text is not hindered.

Daniel Migliore posits that the basis of the Christian faith is not *what must I know,* but *what must I do and who must I be* in order to be saved. I conclude with his statement as a springboard for my favor of and affinity for narrative theology, which tells the story of the Christian faith, consequently telling us who we are in Christ!

Bibliography

1. Barth, Karl. *Church Dogmatics.* 13 vols. Edinburgh: T. & T. Clark, 1936–1969.

2. Fodor, James. *Christian Hermeneutics.* New York: Clarendon Oxford Press, 1995.

3. Frei, Hans. *Eclipse of Biblical Narrative.* New Haven: Yale University Press, 1974.

4. Frei, Hans. *Scriptural Authority and Narrative Interpretation.* Philadelphia: Fortress Press, 1987.

5. Frei, Hans. *The Doctrine of Revelation in the Thought of Karl Barth.* New Haven: Yale University Press, 1956.

6. Frei, Hans. *The Identity of Jesus Christ.* Philadelphia: Fortress Press, 1974.

7. Frei, Hans. *Theology and Narrative.* New York: Oxford University Press, 1999.

8. Frei, Hans. *Types of Christian Theology.* New Haven: Yale University Press, 1992.

9. Goldingay, John. *Models for Interpretation of Scripture.* Grand Rapids, MI: Eerdmans Publishing Co., 1995.

10. Green, Garrett. *Scriptural Authority and Narrative Interpretation.* Philadelphia: Fortress Press, 1987.

11. Hauerwas, Stanley and Burrell, David. *Why Narrative.* Eugene, OR: Wipf and Stock Publishers, 1997.

12. Hegel, G. W. F. *Phenomenology of Spirit*. New York: Oxford University Press 1977.

13. Jones, Joe. "Introduction to Theology" (notes, 1998).

14. Lacocque, Andre. *Thinking Biblically: Exegetical and Hermeneutic Studies*. Chicago: University of Chicago Press, 1998.

15. MacArthur, John Jr. *Rediscovering Expository Preaching*. Dallas: Word Publishing, 1992.

16. McGrath, Allister. *Christian Theology: An Introduction*. Oxford, UK: Blackwell Publishers, 1994.

17. Migliore, Daniel. *Faith Seeking Understanding*. Grand Rapids, MI: Eerdmans Publishing, 1991.

18. Poland, Lynn. *The New Criticism, Neoorthodoxy and the New Testament*. Chicago: Chicago Scholars Press, 1985.

19. Ricoeur, Paul. "Philosophy of Religious Language," Journal of Religion 54, (1974).

20. Ricoeur, Paul. *Essays on Biblical Interpretation*. Philadelphia: Fortress Press, 1980.

21. Ricoeur, Paul. *Figuring the Sacred*. Minneapolis: Fortress Press, 1995.

22. Ricoeur, Paul. *Freedom and Nature: The Voluntary and Involuntary*. Evanston, Ill: Northwestern University Press, 1966.

23. Ricoeur, Paul. *Hermeneutics and the Human Sciences*. New York: Cambridge University Press, 1981.

24. Ricoeur, Paul. *History and Truth*. Evanston, Ill: Northwestern University Press, 1965.

25. Ricoeur, Paul. *Husserl: An Analysis of His Phenomenology*. Evanston, Ill: Northwestern University Press, 1967.

26. Ricoeur, Paul. *Interpretation Theory: Discourse and Surplus of Meaning*. Fort Worth: Texas Christian University Press, 1976.

27. Ricoeur, Paul. *Lectures on Ideology and Utopia*. New York: Columbia University Press, 1986.

28. Ricoeur, Paul. *Main Trends in Philosophy*. New York: Holmes and Meier, 1979.

29. Ricoeur, Paul. *The Conflict of Interpretations: Essays in Hermeneutics*. Evanston, Ill: Northwestern University Press, 1974.

30. Ricoeur, Paul. *The Reality of the Historical Past*. Milwaukee: Marquette University Press, 1984.

31. Stroup, George. *The Promise of Narrative Theology*. Eugene, OR: Wipf and Stock, 1997.

32. Wallace, Mark. *The Second Naiveté*. Macon, GA: Mercer University Press, 1990.

33. Williamson, Clark. "Systematic Theology" (notes, 1998).

Vita

Dr. David A. Hampton is Senior Pastor of Bethany Baptist Church of Brooklyn, NY. Dr. Hampton was ordained under the tutelage of Rev. Dr. Jeffrey A. Johnson, Sr. and had successfully served as a senior pastor in Indianapolis from 2000 to 2007, prior to his call to the historic Bethany Baptist Church of Brooklyn, NY in January 2008. He is honored to follow the 43 year pastorate of the late and legendary Rev. Dr. William Augustus Jones, Jr.

Dr. Hampton also served as a Field Education Supervisor at Christian Theological Seminary in 2005. He was a religious columnist for the Indianapolis Recorder Newspaper (the nation's fourth oldest African-American publication), and was a contributing columnist for the Indianapolis Star & News *Focus* Section 2005-07. He is listed among Distinguished Faith Leaders in the 2003-07 editions of Who's Who in Black Indianapolis and the Inaugural Edition of Who's Who in Black New York City in 2009.

Upon his arrival to New York City, Dr. Hampton took seriously the prophetic call of social justice as he participated in a May 2008 protest of the Sean Bell verdict. He was arrested and jailed for civil disobedience. Dr. Hampton currently serves on the Board of Directors of the National Action Network under its President, Rev. Al Sharpton, and in June 2008, was inducted as a member of Brooklyn Congregations Together (BCT) by Rev. Dr. Johnny Ray Youngblood. In October 2008, Dr. Hampton was elected 1st Vice President of the New York State Progressive

Congress of Christian Education, and in 2009 was appointed by PNBC President Dr. T. Dewitt Smith to serve as Chairman of the Committee on Internal Affairs for the Progressive National Baptist Convention. In his passion for education, Dr. Hampton serves on the Board of Directors of Bedford Prep Charter High School, and on the Advisory Board of Boys and Girls High School—both in the Bedford Stuyvesant area of Brooklyn, NY.

Dr. Hampton earned a B.A. degree in Criminal Justice from the University of Indianapolis, a Master of Theological Studies Degree, and a Doctor of Ministry Degree in Practical Theology (Summa Cum Laude) from Christian Theological Seminary.

He is a member of Omega Psi Phi Fraternity, husband of wife (Hope), and father of two children (Taylor, 14 and Gabriel, 4).

Made in the USA
Lexington, KY
04 January 2011